Post Cards
from
Old Kansas City II

By Mrs. Sam Ray

Historic
Kansas City
Foundation

The publication of this book was made possible by Mrs. Sam Ray through the generous use of her postcard collection and text. Financial support came from the Mason L. Dean Trust at Boatmen's First National Bank of Kansas City, private donors, and the Historic Kansas City Foundation.

All proceeds from this book benefit the Historic Kansas City Foundation education and publications fund.

Published by Historic Kansas City Foundation
Edited by Doran L. Cart
Printed by Ashcraft, Inc.
Cover photograph by E.G. Schempf

The first publication in book form of Mrs. Sam Ray's newspaper articles on post-cards of Kansas City's history, *Post Cards from Old Kansas City*, produced by Historic Kansas City Foundation in 1980, proved popular beyond expectation.

The book represented nostalgia, provoked thought, pleased the eye, and won awards. It eventually sold out of print. Mrs. Ray, however, continued writing her column for the Kansas City *Times* and the interest in these history-packed pieces of cardboard continued as well. Mrs. Ray's extensive collection of hundreds of postcards, relating to Kansas City and elsewhere, also grew.

A casual meeting in late winter, 1986, with Mrs. Ray, Dave Boutros of the Western Historical Manuscript Collection and Historic Kansas City Foundation staff led to the discussion of possible publication of another volume of postcards of historic Kansas City.

From the earliest talks throughout the card selection process, one point remained clear for all concerned. The book should be like the newspaper articles, informative and historical, and the postcards should remain in a newsprint context. The book was not to be an art book, but a history book, using the postcards as documents, remnant views of past events, people and buildings. Some lithographic cards are in color, but many of the original images used are photographic postcards in black and white.

The historical information Mildred Ray gathered to write about the postcards and what they represent appeared in the Kansas City *Times* and the Kansas City *Star* from the years 1968 to 1987. It is lively, personal and timely. Mrs. Ray's people were pioneers in Kansas City. She is a resource of the area's heritage. Her recollections, research and concern for Kansas City, old and new, are in each paragraph.

So, enjoy!

Doran L. Cart
Historic Kansas City Foundation
August 1987, Kansas City, Missouri

113—Hotel Phillips, Kansas City, Mo.

The 20-story, 450 room Hotel Phillips was Kansas City's tallest hotel when it was finished in February, 1931 at 12th & Baltimore.

It had another distinction. The hostelry was completed and ready for occupancy according to contract in one year's time. This time included the razing of the Glennon Hotel and excavating to much deeper levels for the larger building.

Not a single day of work was lost because of weather or labor disputes. On completion, an article stated:

"Music was on tap in every room of the hotel from any one of the four local radio stations. Last minute jobs by decorators, plumbers, painters, carpet layers and men installing drapery fixtures were finished to gay music, with no complaints from the many subcontractors nor the Phillips Building Company. All seemed imbued with the same spirit, pride in finishing the new hotel in the contracted time of one year."

Architectural plans for the structure were drawn up by Boillot & Lauck. The lobby was unique, with black glass used effectively on the ceiling to give an impression of space. There were several dining rooms, and the Pioneer Room, seating 300, was used for large dinners and meetings. Murals in it were by Daniel MacMorris.

Charles E. Phillips, president of the hotel company, had come to Kansas City when he was 15 from his farm home at New Cambria, Mo. He erected more than a score of hotels and apartments here.

This early promotional card shows a drawing of the Savoy Hotel at 9th and Central. It was built in two sections, the east in 1888, the west in 1906. Originally, the west entrance was used exclusively by ladies.

The artist of the sketch used a bit of artistic license to give symmetry to the picture by adding several extra rooms on the south side. The structure is actually not as deep.

The hotel grill room was limited to male guests. Women could use the main dining room.

The original woodwork, stained glass windows, high-backed mirrored bar, marble floors and embossed tin ceilings remain in the renowned Savoy Grill to give current patrons an aura of days gone by.

HOTEL SAVOY, KANSAS CITY HOTEL SAVOY CO., FRANK P. EWINS, PREST.

Harris House Hotel in Westport, built in 1844; stopping place of Boone, Scott, Fremont, Houston, Benton, Pike, Carson, Bridger. Headquarters Santa Fe Trail traffic; battle Westport was directed by Brigadier General Curtis from roof of this house.
Copyright 1912

The Harris House Hotel, located in the center of the town of Westport at Pennsylvania Avenue and Westport Road, was built in 1844 and kept by John Harris.

It was known far and wide for its generous hospitality and Southern cooking. Early patrons of the hostelry were the Santa Fe Trail outfitters, the wagon masters, government sutlers and factors, for Westport was a terminus.

Travelers of note who stayed at the Harris House included General Fremont, Senator Benton, Washington Irving and Horace Greeley. General Fremont left his wife, Jessie, at the hotel for months at a time while he made expeditions in the far west.

The old hotel served as General Curtis' headquarters during the Battle of Westport, and from its roof he could survey a wide area.

Today the site of the old hotel is occupied by a parking lot and new structures.

Kansas City's newest and largest apartment hotel, the Bellerive 214 E. Armour Boulevard (200 apartments, some with 5 rooms), formally opened on November 9, 1922, with a preview dinner given by the St. Louis owners, A.N. Cornwell, his brother F.M. Cornwell, and Charles Bland.

The hotel, designed by Preston J. Bradshaw, was similar to the Melbourne at Grand and Lindell in St. Louis. There was a spacious lobby and six dining rooms, one public and five private.

Early residents recalled a gracious lifestyle in the hotel's early years. Four maids were assigned to each floor day and night. The night maids took care of turn-downs in each bedroom and placed a small glass pitcher of ice water on each night stand.

Guests were not permitted to go up on the front elevator with packages. Upon entering the hotel, packages were handed to the doorman, who in turn gave them to the bellman, who

Bellerive Hotel, Kansas City, Mo.

took them up in the service elevator.

Many celebrities stayed at the Bellerive over the years, including Mary Pickford and Buddy Rogers, Jeanette McDonald, Lillian and Dorothy Gish and Dame Edith Sitwell, and the British ambassador, Lord Inverchapel, and his lady.

The 5-story brick building pictured here was listed in the city directory of 1895 as the "Navarro Block" on the northwest corner of 12th and Baltimore. There were apartments upstairs and shops below.

Plans were made in June, 1919, to convert the building into a modern hotel. E.F. Geraughty, an experienced hotel man, took a ten-year lease on the hostelry at an annual rate of $25,000. "Glennon Hotel" was the new name.

A Kansas City *Star* story publicizing the transaction said, "Mr. Geraughty's lease does not embrace five storerooms on the ground floor, but gives him a first floor lobby and offices and 98 guest rooms. The rates of the new hotel will range from $2 to $5 a day."

One of the "ground floor storerooms" referred to was leased by two recently returned World War I veterans, Harry S. Truman and Eddie Jacobson. The 1920 City Directory states: "Truman and Jacobson, Inc., Harry S. Truman, Edw. Jacobson, men's furng. 104 W. 12th."

After about two year's operation,

the postwar depression brought an end to the clothing shop. By 1922, Jacobson was selling shirts on the road and Truman had entered the political arena.

The Glennon Hotel operated until 1929, when it was razed to make room for the 20-story Phillips Hotel.

The old Glennon Hotel has long since been forgotten. Perhaps there is little cause for it to be remembered, unless, of course, one notes that here was the place from which a Missouri farm boy took his first steps toward becoming President of the United States.

The Centropolis Hotel at the northwest corner of 5th and Grand was a popular place after it was built in 1880. The builder, Moses Broadwell, came here from Mississippi.

Major William Gilpin, a friend of Broadwell, suggested the hotel be called the Centropolis. Since Gilpin, a West Pointer, mapmaker and highly respected authority on the city and its relation to the Western Plains, was one of Kansas City's earliest boosters, his choice of names was accepted. Whitney's History stated: "As far back as 1859 William Gilpin made a map, lithographed in St. Louis, showing Kansas City or Centropolis, as he named it, because it was so near the geographical center of the U.S., to be a great center of commerce, and prophesied for it a glorious future."

At the grand opening of the hotel "two fine bands played for dancing and the canvassed floor resounded with the merry patter of a thousand feet. Only sunrise stopped the festivities."

The Centropolis was the first hotel in the city to install electric lighting.

As the city moved southward and new hotels were built, the old Centropolis faded. When it was razed in 1941, a news story described past glories:

"The Centropolis Hotel was a rendezvous for midnight suppers after the ball. Its red-carpeted lobby felt the mighty tread of John L. Sullivan.... The house once sheltered General Grant, Presidents Arthur and Cleveland. Here W.J. Bryan stayed when he first ran for President."

The postcard was mailed in March 1906.

Five of the world's greatest military and naval leaders are pictured at the Liberty Memorial ground-breaking dedication in 1921. From left to right, Baron Jacques of Belgium, General Diaz of Italy, Marshal Foch of France, General Pershing, commander of the American Expeditionary Force, and Admiral Beatty of Great Britain.

The postcard was first printed in the newspaper in 1980 at the request of John H. Bullard of Jackson, Tennessee, a member of the 129th Field Artillery, Battery D, which was under the command of Captain Harry S. Truman. Bullard wrote:

"I hope you have a copy of the immortal picture of the dedication of the Liberty Memorial . . .

Moxie Hanley of the Hanley Photo Company at 10th and McGee took this picture. I saw Moxie take the picture from a vantage point by climbing a loudspeaker stationed near the podium.

Captain Truman and several others of our old outfit were there, along with members of the 42nd Division, the old Rainbow Division, and also numbers of the 89th Division....

Spectators massed in front of Union Station (with some on the roof) in this photographic postcard at the time of the 1921 American Legion Convention in Kansas City.

The huge crowd was gathered to hear dedication speeches for the ground breaking of the proposed Liberty Memorial, just south of the station.

KANSAS CITY, MO.
American Legion Fountain
Ninth and Main Streets

The American Legion fountain was dedicated Nov. 3, 1921 at 9th and Main Streets.

Robert Merrell Gage, Kansas City sculptor, designed the stone memorial and fountain. Gage's design included bronze insets of figures of World War I in action, recessed into a pillar topped by four stern eagles. Local architects assisted in the design.

The memorial was relocated later to the Budd Park Esplanade, on the east side of Van Brunt Boulevard at Anderson. A list of Kansas City American Legion posts named for men who gave their lives was also included on the monument.

"William T. Fitzsimmons, Murray Davis, William J. Bland, Joseph Dillon, Arthur Maloney, Sanford M. Brown Jr., James Cummings, Joseph Liebman, Hewitt Swearingen, Wayne Minor."

The first week of November, 1921, 60,000 World War I veterans and servicemen marched through the streets of Kansas City while the military leaders of the Allied Nations looked on. The occasion was the national convention of the American Legion and the dedication of the site of the Liberty Memorial.

The public schools of Greater Kansas City were dismissed for the day and pupils with their teachers rode the street cars to designated curbside spots along the line of march.

Madame Ernestine Schumann-Heink, idol of the Legion, opened the convention, which was held in Convention Hall, by singing the "Star Spangled Banner." She held an American flag which she waved during dramatic moments of the anthem.

AMERICAN LEGION PARADE KANSAS CITY, MO. 1921
(DOUBLEDAY) '7'

THE LIBERTY
MEMORIAL

KANSAS CITY'S TRIBUTE
TO THE BOYS

A 21-gun salute greeted President Calvin Coolidge and Mrs. Coolidge as they appeared outside Union Station November 11, 1926. They were here to dedicate Kansas City's newly finished 2 million dollar Liberty Memorial erected "for those who served in the World War in defense of liberty and our country."

Another 21-gun salute was fired when the President reached the platform at the base of the 200-foot limestone shaft, with its "pillar of cloud by day and pillar of flame by night."

A throng of 150,000 at the memorial heard the President's forty minute address – the largest crowd he had ever addressed, according to a Kansas City *Times* story the following day.

Her majesty, Queen Marie, consort of King Ferdinand of Romania, with her children, Prince Nicholas and Princess Ileana, were also honored guests at the dedication.

Queen Marie played a behind-the-scenes role in strengthening the pro-Allied factions in Romania during the World War. Her popularity with the troops was high. Queen Marie died in 1938.

During her short stay in Kansas City, the queen rode with her children in the Armistice Day parade; laid a wreath on the memorial and spoke a few words of appreciation to a huge crowd and radio audience; attended a concert at the pavilion and was royally entertained at the Jacob Loose home on Armour Boulevard.

Two months later, an item from the *Times* stated the queen's visit to Kansas City cost the city a sum of $762.05.

The Erste Deutsche Methodisten Kirche (First German Methodist Church) at the northeast corner of 14th and Campbell was first listed in the city directory of 1885. The pastor's home was next door east. Services were conducted in German and the church was packed on Sundays with young German immigrants who had come to Kansas City to work. Many were factory, plant, store and domestic employees.

The church rendered a tremendous service to its parishioners during the period of transition from German customs and language to American ways.

The postcard was mailed from Kansas City by Minnie Schowengerdt Minich to her friend, Mrs. Carrie Osborn in Williamsville, Mo., in 1909, wishing her a "Happy New Year" for the coming year of 1910. The Schowengerdts were members of the church and drove by horse and buggy from their farm south of Independence to attend services. Later the large Schowengerdt family founded a new German Methodist church, built in 1893, at Lexington and Spring in Independence.

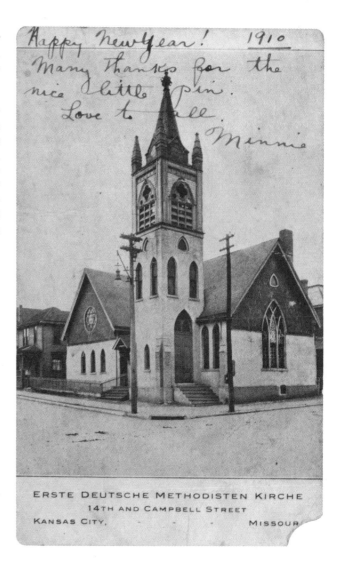

ERSTE DEUTSCHE METHODISTEN KIRCHE
14TH AND CAMPBELL STREET
KANSAS CITY,   MISSOURI

Prospect Ave. Congregational Church.
Kansas City, Mo.

The first services held at the newly finished Prospect Avenue Congregational Church at 29th and Prospect were conducted on the morning of July 21, 1907, by the pastor, Rev. Dr. E.F. Schwab. (Mayor Beardsley was the speaker at the evening services.)

The completion of the new church designed by Rudolf Markgraf, resulted from the work of a faithful little band of earnest church workers who had been worshipping in a hall at 26th and Prospect.

Work on the building, which cost $35,000, was begun in 1906 and the congregation, numbering about 200, began their tenure in the new church practically out of debt.

The old Prospect Avenue stone church is being used by the Metropolitan African Methodist Episcopal Zion Church.

H-1602   LINWOOD BOULEVARD CHRISTIAN CHURCH, KANSAS CITY MO.

The Linwood Boulevard Christian Church, with the Atkins Hall Memorial building at the rear, is shown on this 1915 postcard. The building was constructed of Phoenix stone, an almost white material, and the roof was of red tile. Henry F. Hoit was the architect.

The church as shown was finished and dedicated December 26, 1909. The J.B. and Mary Atkins memorial was added in 1914.

Dr. Jenkins, the pastor, was a progressive liberal. His church doors were open to all creeds and denominations, and little attention was paid to old church forms and rituals. Dances and movies were held in the church parlors in 1927. There were objections and controversy over this and eventually the dances were held at the Armory on Main Street. Sunday night movies were continued.

Liberal policies under Dr. Jenkins resulted in the exclusion of the congregation from the co-operative circle of other Christian churches in the city.

The church was destroyed by fire November 1, 1939. Church rolls and financial records were saved by Miss Margaret LaMar, the church secretary.

A new site at 4601 Main Street, overlooking the Plaza, was chosen for rebuilding. Frank Lloyd Wright created the initial design for the church.

The old site on Linwood was later occupied by an A. & P. food store and parking lot.

The First Church of Christ, Scientist, at 9th and Forest, was the first of its denomination west of the Mississippi.

Mary Baker Eddy established the Massachusetts Metaphysical College in 1881. Five years later a graduate of the school, Mrs. Emma D. Behan, came to Kansas City and opened an office in her home at 913 East 14th Street.

Later Second and Third churches were formed (before 1900) and in 1897, the three churches united under the Charter of 1890 and plans were made for building a church. Arthur E. Stilwell, of railroad fame, was an active spirit in the enterprise.

The stately early-Gothic stone structure with terra cotta roofing and low, square towers, as pictured on the German-made post card, was built at a cost of $67,000 and was considered one of the most beautiful in this part of the country.

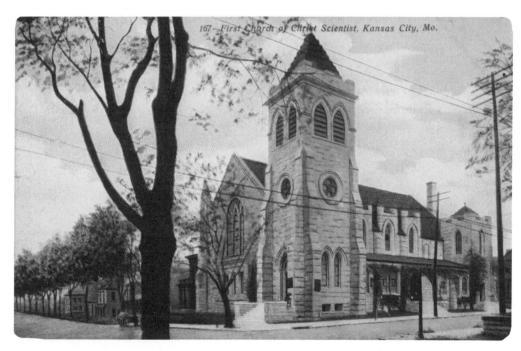

167—First Church of Christ Scientist, Kansas City, Mo.

Early-day homes shown on Forest Street are no longer standing, having been replaced by apartment houses.

The old church, mellowed by decades of uninterrupted services, still stands.

9

Geo. B. Peck Dry Goods Co's. Building. Kansas City, Mo.

The George B. Peck Dry Goods Company was formerly the "Doggett Store Co.," owned by John Doggett, early-day merchant who opened his first store in Kansas City in 1866.

A son of an affluent Detroit merchant and banker, George B. Peck, came west in 1889 and he soon bought a block of stock in the Doggett store, immediately taking an active part in the management. He had learned merchandising in Detroit under his father's tutelage and in other Eastern emporiums.

Peck served as director and vice-president before buying out Doggett's interest in the store in 1898. The Directors voted in 1901 to change the name of the company to George B. Peck Dry Goods.

Peck was known for his charities and good works for his employees. Before the store installed overhead wires carrying baskets with purchases and money, young boys and girls were employed to run with these items to a central cashier. After making a sale, the clerk would cry "Cash!" and a runner would quickly appear.

Schooling proved rather sketchy for these young employees who needed the jobs and preferred them to school. Peck established a school in one corner of the carpet room for them. He furnished books and stationery and paid the teachers. Class hours were from 8:00 a.m. to 10:00 a.m.

The Peck Dry Goods store closed early in 1964 after 77 years of operation. In September, 1964, Foreman-Clark leased the Main Street building for many years.

Jaccards' clock "out front" was a familiar downtown landmark shown in this early photographic postcard of Jaccards' Jewelry Store in its second Kansas City location at 1034 Main, next door to the old John Taylor Dry Goods Company. Show windows displayed china-globed lamps, punch bowls, vases and a cut glass water bottle.

Eugene G.E. Jaccard and Walter M. Jaccard, sons of D.C. Jaccard, left their father's St. Louis firm in 1888 and established a jewelry store in Kansas City at 815 Main. The firm moved to its third location at 1017 Walnut in 1906. Other stores were later established in the Country Club Plaza and the Ward Parkway Shopping Center. The store depicted was later demolished.

JACCARD, JEWELER AND ART STATIONER, 1034 MAIN ST.

At the silk department of John Taylor's Dry Goods Company, long-skirted customers with sailor hats topping their pompadours shopped for material by the yard.

While they rested on stools at the counter, 12 male clerks and 2 floor walkers were ready to give counsel and suggestions regarding the crisp taffetas, chiffons and silks suitable for dresses and skirts. Women's clothing at the time of the image was almost entirely made at home or by the dressmaker.

John Taylor's was operated on a strictly cash basis at the time, a fact of which both customer and owner were proud.

John Taylor's was founded in 1881 and was purchased by Macy's in 1947 after which an expansion and rebuilding program more than doubled the size of the store.

SILK DEPARTMENT
JOHN TAYLOR D.G. Co.
KANSAS CITY, MO.

THE LARGEST EXCLUSIVE RETAIL SHOE DEALERS IN THE WORLD.

G. R. KINNEY CO. INC., 814-816-818 DELAWARE ST., KANSAS CITY, MO.

The Delaware Building, located just north of the old junction (where Main and Delaware met at 9th), first appears in the city directory at 812-820 Delaware.

In the 1913 promotional postcard, made for the G.R. Kinney & Co. Shoe Store, a store front apparently has been sliced off of each side of the building so that only the Kinney store would be pictured, numbers 814, 816 and 818. 812 and 820 are missing.

A sign on the store front reads "Big Value 98¢" and another tells of a more expensive shoe, "Great Value $1.65."

The electric street lamp at the front of the store shows the new lights installed in Kansas City the year before.

The Frank Tilk Ornamental Iron Works designed the pole and fixture. The brackets (minus the top or fifth globe) were placed on trolly car poles on streets used by street car lines.

G.R. Kinney Shoes were sold at the Delaware Street building from 1913 until 1930.

11

Hope the collection is growing....write soon

Kansas City, Mo.   1520 The Owl Drug Store

Right this way to get your ice-cream sodas
B.M.S.

The Owl Drug Store, occupying two store buildings fronting on the west side of Main Street between 9th and 10th Streets, is shown on a postcard mailed from Kansas City July 12, 1907 to Miss Mame Slater at the Woodcroft Sanitarium, Pueblo, Colo.

The reverse side of the card gives an insight into the postal responsibilities of that day. In addition to the usual circular postmarks, there is an oval postmark, evidently stamped by the mail clerk on the westbound train, which reads: "Train late, mail delayed." How thoughtful – and all for a one-cent gren postage stamp.

The Owl Drug Store owners were James and Thomas O'Reilly, who had been hardware merchants in Independence, MO. The hardware business was slow so they opened a drug store. They first started with $1800 in stock in the old Warder-Grand Theater on East 9th Street. One brother ran the store in the day and the other took charge at night.

About 1890, the O'Reillys moved to 920 Main, renting the storeroom at $150 a month. They began new merchandising policies, cut prices and used extensive advertising.

By 1926, when the brothers, both in their 60s, sold out to a San Francisco drug firm, there were Owl Drug Stores listed at four downtown locations.

The interior view of the Owl Drug Store was mailed in 1909.

The building on Main was razed.

CENTURY THEATRE, KANSAS CITY, MO.

Pub. by Paul Eskenasy, Kansas City, Mo.

The Century Theater at 12th and Central Streets, designed by Louis S. Curtiss, prominent Kansas City architect, was first called the Standard.

The Standard Theater opened in September, 1900, offering performances of burlesque comedy and vaudeville.

After a January 31, 1901, fire destroyed the Coates Opera House three blocks away, the bill included opera and comic performances transferred to the Standard from the ashes of the Coates. It was at this time that such popular performers as Sarah Bernhardt, Maude Adams and Richard Mansfield appeared.

In 1902, the theater's name changed to the Century. Burlesque shows scheduled on the Empire circuit presented Al Jolson, Fannie Brice and Eddie Foy.

The Shubert Borthers purchased the theater in 1923 and renamed it Shubert's Missouri. During this era the theater produced legitimate drama.

The theater was intermittently open for touring shows and movies until it closed in 1932. Five years later it was auctioned for back taxes.

In 1941, the theater reopened as the Folly with strip tease shows. Later, X-rated movies were added. It closed again in December, 1973.

The building was placed on the National Register of Historic Places in 1974 because of its importance as an element in the history of Kansas City architecture, society and humanities.

A grass-roots effort saved the building from demolition and after extensive restoration it once again opened for performances and public events, a source of public pride.

The imposing Gillis Opera House owed its existence to the philanthropy of Mrs. Mary A. Gillis Troost.

Mrs. Troost was a niece of William Gillis, one of the 14 original members of the town company of Kansas (later Kansas City, Mo.) and she inherited her uncle's entire estate at his death.

Mrs. Troost died in 1872 and when her will was probated it became known that she had directed a theater to be built in Kansas City with the income from the theater to go toward the maintenance of a home for children, the Gillis Orphan's Home.

It was finally completed in 1883, at the southwest corner of Fifth and Walnut, at a cost of $140,000.

Opening night was September 10, 1883, and it was one of the city's most important social events. Seats sold from 50 cents in the top gallery to $20 for the most expensive boxes.

The Theater drew the top stars and attractions. It was a mecca of lovers of the opera for miles around Kansas City.

An explosion and fire destroyed

Gillis Opera House. Kansas City, Mo.

the theater and 14 shops in June, 1925. A new fireproof brick and stone building with storerooms and a motion picture theater was built on the site in 1926.

In 1969, the rented storerooms continued to help support the Gillis Home, by then located on Wornall Road.

Foyer, Newman Theater, Kansas City, Mo.

Promenade, Newman Theater, Kansas City, Mo.

The site of the Newman Theater was that of the old Brady Building, which had been gutted by fire in 1918. The Newman was the largest motion picture theater to be built in the downtown district and the most costly theater of any sort to be erected here. It was built on a 100-foot frontage at 1114-18 Main Street just 25 feet north of 12th Street. Frank L. Newman's other downtown theaters were the Royal, one-half block north, and the Regent at 109 E. 12th Street.

The architect for the Newman Theater was Alexander Drake. The steel and concrete fireproof building cost nearly $400,000. Seating capacity was 2000. The orchestra pit accommodated a 35-piece orchestra and on special occasions, 50 musicians would be employed.

A large mezzanine floor promenade was located between the first floor and balcony.

Frank Newman left Kansas City in June, 1925, after 11 profitable years operating the theaters. He went to manage theaters in Los Angeles for the famous Players-Lasky Film Corporation. They paid him $900,000 for the Newman and Royal. Many of his employees followed him to California.

In later years, the Newman Theater was called the Paramount and still later, the Towne. It was demolished for a parking lot.

National Bank of Commerce Building, Kansas City, Missouri

An energetic group of men with capital of $20,000 formed the Kansas City Savings Association in April, 1865, occupying a small building near the river front at 2nd and Main Streets. The association was the predecessor of the Commerce Trust Company.

In 1881, Dr. W.S. Woods, a practicing physician, bought the controlling interest in the bank and became its president.

Through a series of mergers and changes in name, the bank eventually became the Commerce Trust Company. A new 16-story building, at 10th and Walnut Streets, was occupied by the bank in 1907. Designed by Jarvis Hunt, it was one of the first and finest skyscrapers in the growing city and had many innovations, including a barber shop, beauty shop, high-speed elevators and a roof-garden luncheon club.

Throughout the years, the handsome building has been frequently modernized, inside and out. It has been connected with the Commerce Towers.

Spring Valley Park, lying in a natural canyon and once the site of an old rock quarry, had six springs bursting from its limestone walls when it was taken over by the park board in 1902. Hundreds drank the cool, refreshing waters which joined to form a small lake, especially enjoyed by ice-skaters in winter.

The irregularly-shaped park at 27th Street and Woodland Avenue contained 33 acres acquired in two parcels and was connected to Troost Park by a strip of land purchased in 1930.

Springs and lake soon disappeared, but the park later boasted picnic facilities, playground equipment and baseball fields.

And there I know a quiet nook
Where passers seldom sally,
A little bench beneath a tree
O won't you steal away with me
To learn, but not from any book
The sweetness of Spring Valley.
– Anonymous, Kansas City *Star*, 1912

Spring, Spring Valley Park, Kansas City, Mo.

Downtown Kansas City was once a series of clay hills dotted here and there with homes. On Baltimore Avenue the topography was particularly irregular.

A chapter, "The Newer Kansas City," in Whitney's 1908 *History of Kansas City* tells of the first development of 10th Street.

"The transformation of 10th Street began in 1906 when the First National Bank began the erection of its elegant new building at the northeast corner of 10th Street and Baltimore Avenue . . .

The building was erected at a cost of $350,000. The exterior of the building is of pure white selected Georgia stone and six magnificent columns stand on the 10th Street side. The interior is finished in white marble.

The building is three stories high and built on the steel skeleton plan. Bronze doors 13 feet in height guard the entrances. The counters are made of marble and the cages of bronze.

The building is fireproof and each desk is provided with a fireproof locker to protect important papers and letters."

The postcard was made in 1907, the year the bank moved into its new quarters.

10th STREET, EAST FROM BALTIMORE, KANSAS CITY, MO.

Main Street Theatre, Kansas City, Mo.

The Mainstreet Theater at the southwest corner of 14th and Main Streets opened October 30, 1921. The popular vaudeville and movie house with a seating capacity of 3000 (designed by renowned theater architects Rapp and Rapp of Chicago) was the first theater in Kansas City to have a nursery for children whose parents were attending the show.

It was quite an experiment in that pre-feminist day, when babies and their mothers were almost inseparable.

A theatre historian related that, "it even had an elephant cage, a pool for seals and an elevator large enough and powerful enough to haul elephants to the stage. Noted performers such as Cab Calloway, Charlie Chaplin, Sir Henry Lauder and Olson & Johnson all head-lined at the vaudeville house."

Records put show attendance three months after the theater opened at an average of 4000 daily, including daytime and evening performances.

Steam and smoke rise from railroad engines at the Union Station on an early Fred Harvey postcard in color.

Passengers make their way north on Main Street on the way to hotels or downtown stores.

The legend on the reverse side reads: 'The steel sheds at the new Union Station, Kansas City, are 1400 feet long and cover an area of 430,000 square feet. They afford space for 32 trains at one time.

This view was made from the Main Street Viaduct which leads street railway traffic directly over the train sheds . . . .''

80079   NEW UNION STATION FROM MAIN ST. VIADUCT, KANSAS CITY, MO.   COPR. FRED HARVEY.

SO WE'LL MEET AGAIN

BUY MORE WAR BONDS

The American Red Cross maintained a canteen in Kansas City at 1021 McGee Street during World War II. The facility was used by soldiers and sailors on leave from duty or passing through the city to military bases in the U.S. or overseas.

Many of the young servicemen who enjoyed the hospitality of the canteen, dropped postcards of appreciation after leaving the city. Some kept in touch even after going overseas.

This card was mailed with a free soldier's stamp from Pvt. Thomas F. Melvin, 33579325, 164 Signal Photo Co., Camp Crowder, Mo., to ''Mrs. Marie Rowland, Hospitality Chairman, Kansas City Canteen....''

It reads, ''Nov. 15, 1943. Esteemed Mrs. Rowland: No I can't keep it to myself – I've got to tell you what I know. You are doing a swell job! And be sure, we boys appreciate your sincere efforts.

My trip, hitch-hiking back to camp, was pretty tedious...but I did get there! Thank you ever so much for making my pass spent in K.C. a time long to be remembered! Cheerio! Yours, Thomas.''

The postcard, published in color, was issued by the U.S. Treasury Department War Savings Staff.

The Board of Trade Building, with its tall, decorative tower at 210 W. 8th, was the prize-winning design of John Wellborn Root of the Chicago firm of architects, Burnham and Root.

Root, who pioneered in developing the American skyscraper, was one of 53 architects who submitted plans in 1886 to the Board of Trade for their office building. It was said that the erection of the impressive seven-story red brick structure, during the years 1886-1888, celebrated the importance of grain in Kansas City.

The first grain market in the city in 1869 occupied a one-room trading hall in the West Bottoms. Corn in wagon-load lots was the main commodity, with wheat secondary. All transactions were handled on a cash basis.

The building pictured was the center of grain trading between 1887 and 1925.

It was demolished in 1968 for a surface parking lot.

BOARD OF TRADE, KANSAS CITY, MO.

East View from City Point, Kansas City, Mo.

"East View from City Point" was made from the top of the bluff at Scarritt Point. Early residents of the East Bottoms below included Belgian and German farmers who were drawn to the fertile Missouri River Valley.

Ferdinand Heim of East St. Louis came to Kansas City with his family in 1884, and in 1887 he and his three eldest sons, Ferdinand, Joe and Mike, purchased 10 acres that included a factory building. They soon erected a malt house and remodeled the old factory into dry cellars. Other buildings were added to the brewery complex. A two-story bottling building at 501 N. Montgall was erected in 1901, designed by architect Charles Smith.

A fire station, constructed for the brewery, was later used by the city. It still stands.

Troost Ave., North
from Linwood and Troost,
Kansas City, Mo.

Troost Avenue, lined with automobiles, many of them Model T Fords, are shown in this 1920s scene looking north toward 31st Street.

The Rossington apartments are in the right background. The Westover office building, also on the east side, furnished space to many of the city's leading doctors and dentists.

Other businesses on the east side of Troost as listed by directories of the '20s were Westover Chocolate Shop; Strauss Peyton Studio; Mary A. Dougherty, millinery; Barclay Corset Shop; Epperly-Crane, corsets; Michelson Building; Prudential Life Insurance Company; National Benevolent Society and Swyden Rug and Drapery Co.

The west side of the street shows the new Joseph Wirthman Building housing Wirthman's Drugstore on the corner and the offices of many doctors and dentists, along with the Isis Theater, built in 1918; the Isis Cafeteria, in the basement at 3104; Louise Winter Millinery Shop; Mary Lane Dry Goods; Humfield-Orear Floral Co.; Martha Washington Candy; Dinty Moore's Restaurant; Baldwin Piano; and the Monkey Steam Dye Works.

The Missouri River steamboat *Kate Swinney* brought Kansas City's first fire engine to the Main Street docks in the late 1860s. The engine was christened "John Campbell" after a local citizen who had done much to establish the first company.

By 1907, the Fire Department began to convert from horse-drawn engines to motor-driven vehicles. Many hated to see the passing of the horse-drawn wagon. Even the horses let go of the era reluctantly, for long after famed team horse "Dan" was retired, he would race across Swope Park grasses whenever he heard a bell.

The postcard titled "Famous Petticoat Lane, Kansas City, Mo.," pictures pedestrians watching a horse-drawn fire engine as it turns north at 11th and Walnut Streets.

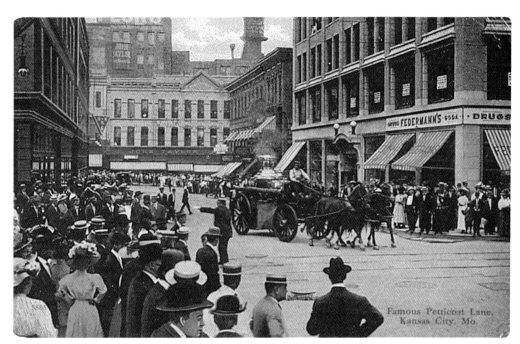

Famous Petticoat Lane,
Kansas City, Mo.

Eighth Street, looking west from Walnut, in the late 1890s held August Zorn's 2-story brick saloon, with striped awnings and Anheuser-Busch signs, at the corner. The city directory at the time listed other businesses in the block: A.T. Rickmers, Gunsmith, Watches and Clocks, Jewelry Repaired; Steam Dye Works; Laundry; Old Hats Made New; Electric Baths; Cigar Factory and Rock Island Ticket Office, 727 Main, with A.H. Moffet, passenger agent, and C.W. Jones, city ticket agent.

In the background of the image are three of Kansas City's finest early office buildings: the Board of Trade, American Bank Building and the Heist Building, with its beehive tower and flag staff.

None of the buildings in the postcard remain.

Kansas City, Mo, 8th Street looking West.

THE KIRK ARMOUR RESIDENCE, KANSAS CITY, MO.

The palatial Kirk Armour home, with the appearance of a French chateau, was built in 1896 at the corner of Warwick and Armour Boulevards.

Armour Boulevard was named for Kirk's uncle, S.B. Armour, a member of the first Kansas City Park Board.

This residence was the largest and most admired architecturally on Armour Boulevard. A great barn to the rear stabled fine horses and was well staffed with grooms and a coachman. Often remembered was the great elm tree in the back yard, where a long cable from the treetop to the ground, straddled by a pulley and rope, furnished fun and breathless rides for the young Armour boys and their friends.

In 1881, Kirk married Miss Anna P. Hearne of Wheeling, W. Va. They occupied homes on Quality Hill, before building the mansion pictured. Armour served as vice-president and general manager of the Armour Packing Company here. At the death of S.B. Armour in 1898, he became president.

The old mansion was later occupied by a school of the French sisters of Notre Dame de Sion. The site was later covered by the Standard Oil office building.

FISHING TACKLE. FIRE ARMS. FIRE WORKS.
CUTLERY. ATHLETIC GOODS & BICYCLES
TALKING MACHINES. KODAKS. TOYS.
1218 SCHMELZER ARMS CO. 1214

SCHMELZER'S NEW UP-TOWN STORE
1214 TO 1218 GRAND AVENUE
KANSAS CITY, MO.

Schmelzer's new "up-town" store, 1214-18 Grand, replaced an earlier store at 710-720 Main.

The store founder was John F. Schmelzer, German-born manufacturer of firearms, who came to America from Oldenburg, Germany in 1844 and settled in Hartford, Conn., where he was associated with Colt's armory.

He arrived by Missouri River steamboat at Leavenworth in 1857 and started the business which became Schmelzer Arms Company. His son, Charles, spent his boyhood days in Leavenworth where he attended grade and high school, becoming associated with his father's business at age sixteen. During the 1880s, Charles traveled in the West by wagon, selling firearms and ammunition.

John Schmelzer retired in 1887 and the firm moved from Leavenworth to Kansas City. Incorporated in 1896 with capital of $75,000, by 1907, it had grown to a $300,000 firm. As "J.F. Schmelzer & Sons," the sons were Charles and Herman.

The legend on the reverse side stated that "Schmelzer Arms Co. at 1214 Grand Ave. is the most interesting store in Kansas City." Many citizens of the day would have agreed, especially men interested in hunting and sports.

266 Union Avenue, showing New Albany Hotel, Kansas City, Mo.

The clang of street car gongs, the screech of cable car brakes on the incline down to the depot, the clomp of horse hoofs on pavement, an intermingling of coal smoke from street-level trains, whisky fumes wafting from swinging saloon doors and cooking odors from the kitchen of the old Blossom House, combine in memories of this street, Union Avenue in the West Bottoms, 1908.

The site pictured was opposite the Union Depot, center of rail travel until 1914. Many Easterners arriving on round-trip excursions decided to stay, and scalpers hawked their return tickets at "bargain" prices.

Three hotels, the Blossom House, New Albany, and the Strangers' Hotel are pictured. None remains today.

The Coates House Hotel, Kansas City, Mo.

Construction on the Coates House at Tenth and Broadway was started before the Civil War, but after the foundation was built, work ended.

During the war, the foundation was boarded over and used as a cavalry stable by Van Horn's battalion.

Work on the hotel was resumed in 1866 and it was finished in 1868. The present structure, depicted, replaced an earlier one. It was built in two major phases in 1886-87 and 1889-91. The architects were Henry Van Brunt and Frank Maynard Howe.

The continuous second floor gallery, with iron railings, as pictured on this early 1900 postcard, was used by President Grover Cleveland and his bride as they viewed Kansas City's first Priests of Pallas Parade, October 13, 1887.

The Coates House not only was the leading hotel, but it was a social center because of its facilities for large dinners and parties. Elegant food and drinks were served by waiters in full dress.

Theatrical stars playing at the Coates Theatre, diagonally across Broadway, found the hotel convenient and old hotel registers show such guests as Edwin Booth, Lawrence Barrett, Joseph Jefferson, Lotta Crabtree, the Boston Ideal Opera Company and Richard Mansfield.

Kersey Coates, owner-builder of the hostelry, came west in 1854 as an agent for Philadelphia capitalists, to buy land and make investments. He chose Kansas City over other towns visited and today is considered the man most closely linked to the growth and greatness of Kansas City.

Five street cars dominate the scene on this 1913 postcard. Several automobiles are in view, but no horse-and-buggy traffic.

Stores and shops display large overhanging signs, among them Federman's Drug Store at 11th and Walnut, in the Lillis Building, demolished in 1987. Farther along are signs of the Olney Music Company and Household Fair.

On the right is a sign designating the Altman Building entrance with a hand pointing the way.

Walnut St. North from 12th St., Kansas City, Mo.

FIRE HEADQUARTERS, KANSAS CITY, MO.

5871

Alex Henderson, then first assistant fire chief, is shown at the right-hand-drive wheel of the first automotive fire apparatus used in Kansas City, a Pope Hartford roadster, a chief's car. William Cody Pahlman, his driver, sits beside him.

The car went into service September 1, 1909; before that, Pahlman remembered that he drove the chief to fires in a horse-drawn buggy.

In 1916, the first promotion for bravery ever awarded by the fire and water board was a captaincy to Lieutenant Pahlman for saving the lives of three persons overcome by smoke in a fire near 14th and Main Streets. Alex Henderson became chief of the fire department in 1918.

This postcard was printed by North American Post Card Company of Kansas City for the Pope Hartford company.

398 Fire Chief
Kansas City Mo

The corner of the old Public Library building at 9th and Locust Streets and the Pepper Building across the street are shown in this photograph taken of Kansas City's great Pepper Building fire, May 8, 1907.

The postcard is one of a set of four showing the fire from different vantage points.

The Pepper Building was built around an open court, with balconies on every floor, and the fire, of unknown origin, spread rapidly due to the open construction. The fire was well underway before the alarm was given.

Many of the tenants were music teachers, with studios in the building. In 1970, many Kansas Citians still remembered weekly trips to the building for piano lessons, sometimes by bicycle and carrying round leather cases with their rolled-up music books.

At least 15 persons jumped from windows before fire fighting equipment arrived. Many were injured and taken to hospitals. William Cody Pahlman was the lieutenant on the 3-horse hitch aerial truck. He said the vehicle was unable to maneuver into the narrow alley, so rescues were made from the extension and Pompier (pole-like) ladders.

View at Ninth and Locust Streets, showing part of Public Library, and Pepper Building on the west; stream of water thrown to fifth floor. The Pepper Building Fire, Kansas City, Mo., May 8th, 1907.

Fire Headquarters, Kansas City, Missouri.

The Kansas City Fire Department was the pride of every Kansas Citian when this picture of its headquarters, at 1020 Central Street, was taken after 1907.

George C. Hale was elected fire chief in 1882. Hale was a dedicated and inventive fire fighter. Among his inventions were the Hale water tower, Hale swinging harness, the sliding pole and the Hale tin roof cutter.

In 1893, he and his crew went to England with two of their best horses, Dan and Joe, pure white Arabians, their scaling ladders, and a Hale water tower. There, at the International Fire Congress, they won the first place gold medal in hitching, reaching the scene of fire and throwing water: time, 8 1/2 seconds. In 1900, in Paris, the team won the International Cup.

54:—SOUTHWESTERN BELL TELEPHONE CO. BUILDING. KANSAS CITY, MO.

The 28-story (former) Southwestern Bell Telephone Building at 11th and Oak Streets was not always as tall as it is today.

Ground was broken for the original building in 1917. World War I, and a scarcity of manpower and material, caused a halt in construction and the building was not completed until May, 1920.

The structure was outgrown by the telephone company in less than a decade, and it was necessary to double the size of the building in 1929 by adding 14 more floors.

The 28-story building was ready for use in 1929. Later, the equivalent of two more stories was added with the erection of tall microwave radio relay antennas.

The building pictured underwent extensive "modernization" in later decades and its present day appearance is quite different.

The Sisters of St. Mary, from St. Louis, had done the nursing at the city's German Hospital for 10 years before this 4-story brick hospital at 28th and Main Streets was built for them in 1909.

Howe & Hoit were the architects and the original cost, including the grounds, was $150,000. There were 150 beds, 72 of which were free. A new wing in 1916 added an elaborate chapel on the top floor. Later, a 3-story nurses' home, training school, power plant and laundry were built.

The 7-story St. Mary's hospital built in 1950 was consolidated with the old section and the facility came to cover more than four square blocks. The stone steps and entrance pictured were long ago removed.

St. Mary's Hospital, 28th & Main Sts., Kansas City, Mo.

Masonic Temple,
Ninth and Harrison Streets,
Kansas City, Mo.

The Masonic Temple at Ninth and Harrison Streets was said to be one of the most perfect architecturally, and one of the few temples of a purely Masonic character. Designed by J.C. Sunderland, it was dedicated September 30, 1911.

A large dining hall, seating 400 persons, and a kitchen occupied the first floor. Offices of the secretary and other offices were on the second floor.

The third floor, with its Persian Room, was of "oriental beauty," according to a Kansas City *Journal* story on the dedication day, and the description of the "ornamental beamed ceiling, with electrical bulbs for illumination" indicates that electricity was still a novelty.

An auditorium, with a seating capacity of 1000, was lavishly decorated and halls were lined with light Vermont marble.

The building is still used today and has been restored.

One of Kansas City's oldest school properties, "New Central High" at the southeast corner of 11th and Locust streets is pictured on a postcard, mailed in 1909 to Miss Gladys Brown, Atchison, Kan.

The Board of Education first opened Central High School in rented property, Sept. 17, 1867, on the first floor of the small Starke building, at the same location. Kansas City owned no public school buildings at the time and had no money to erect them. Classes were held in "old deserted buildings, unoccupied store rooms and damp gloomy basements," notes Carrie Whitney's *History of Kansas City*.

In 1868 the school board bought the Starke building and in 1883 a new school building was erected, the first section of Central High, as shown on the right side of the picture. (My mother, Kate Fisher, later a school teacher in Rosedale, Kan., graduated here in the late '80s.)

In 1882 the Starke building was torn down and the four-story red brick structure with the tower, as shown, was built.

The school boasted many nationally known figures as graduates: Gladys Swarthout, lyric soprano; William Powell, movie star, and baseball's Casey Stengel among them. Well remembered are the good basketball teams of both boys and girls.

When Central High moved south in 1915 to its present location at Linwood and Indiana, the old 11th street facility became the home of the Polytechnic Institute and Junior College.

It was later razed and used as a parking lot. Today the historic site of this early public high school is occupied by the Municipal Courts building.

The postcard was published in color by the Elite Postcard Co., of Kansas City.

CITY MARKET, KANSAS CITY, MO.   Pub. by Paul Eskenasy, Kansas City, Mo.

This postcard, mailed here in 1910, shows the old City Market and the red brick City Hall at 4th and Main Streets in the background.

Three street cars, loading and unloading those who have come for the farmers' fresh produce, add to the heavy horse and wagon traffic.

Even before erection of the first market house at this site in 1858, the public square was a busy place. Early in the 19th century, river boats from St. Louis loaded with provisions, ammunition, new settlers and news landed at the nearby Missouri River loading. Early settlers gathered at this point to purchase supplies and either sell or trade their produce, furs and other commodities.

This early Mediterranean style residence at Mission Drive and Overhill Road was home of the late Dr. Sam Roberts, well-known ear, nose and throat specialist.

According to Miller Nichols, this area was originally a rock quarry. Rock was hauled by horse teams and used to build roads in Mission Hills.

Dr. Roberts owned an adjoining site from 1926 and bought the quarry site from the Nichols Company with the idea of developing a rock garden and pool. Hare & Hare, landscape architects, made studies of the rugged spot and a pool was formed and plantings established, with ascending turf carpets broken here and there by jutting rocks. A small summer house with poplar trees at either side was erected near the pool.

The Roberts residence was built in 1930, designed by Texas architects Ayers & Ayers. In 1978, the owners rehabilitated the pool area and restored the original beauty of the rock garden with plantings of flowers and shrubs.

KANSAS CITY, MO. - A Home in Mission Hills

27

A 1931 color postcard pictures the new Kansas City Power & Light Co. Building, 479 feet high, at the northwest corner of Baltimore and 14th Street.

A news story of the day stated, "Fifty years of electrical growth in Kansas City brings us this achievement, Missouri's tallest building ... one of the milestones for the light company under the leadership of Joseph F. Porter."

The structure was surmounted by a 97-foot tower, its apex a gigantic pillar of changing colored lights, glowing at night like a magnificent jewel, and visible miles away.

A license was granted November 14, 1881, by the American Electric Light Co. of Connecticut to several different Kansas Citians. Intense competition marked the early years.

Between 1886 and 1890, Kansas City granted 11 franchises to seven different companies, all permitting the distribution of electrical energy. The result was costly duplication of equipment.

Eventually it was recognized that competing in certain utility fields was against the public interest. The Kansas City Power & Light Co. represented a final merger of these early companies.

M. K. GOETZ BREWING COMPANY -- Kansas City, Missouri

The M.K. Goetz Brewery at the northeast corner of 17th and Indiana, is pictured on this card published about 1936, when the building was completed. The promotional card's back caption adds: "America's most modern brewers. New from the ground up."

Michael Karl Goetz was a German immigrant who stopped at St. Joseph on the way to the California gold fields and decided to stay. He established his own brewery in a small frame building after working a few months for another brewer.

The company started making plans for its Kansas City plant immediately after the repeal of prohibition. Cost of the building was $750,000.

At its peak the brewery, specializing in draught beer, turned out 150,000 barrels annually. As the demand for bottled, canned and packaged beer products increased, Goetz shifted its operation to its main St. Joseph plant. It discontinued brewing operations here in the 1960s.

KANSAS CITY STOCK YARDS, KANSAS CITY, MO.
THE GREATEST STOCK CATTLE MARKET OF THE WORLD. 20,000 PERSONS ARE EMPLOYED HERE.

16th Street in 1876.

The new building provided offices for the stockyards company and commission men besides two banking rooms, a restaurant, billiard hall and barber shop. It afforded for the first time adequate, modern facilities for market operations.

Through the years it was enlarged and improved many times. The postcard pictures the enlarged structure in the early 1900s. It finally occupied two and a half acres of ground, which was partly in Missouri. A line of colored tile across the lobby floor marked the state line.

In June 1903 the great flood swept across the West Bottoms from bluff to bluff to a depth of 15 to 30 feet. Water reached the second floor of the aging building. Afterwards, cracks appeared in the structure and plans were made to replace it.

Today's Livestock Exchange Building at 16th and Genessee was built in 1910.

A stockyards company was organized in Kansas City in 1871 and construction of the yards was completed in time for that year's shipments.

Pens, chutes and other facilities were erected on a tract of 13 1/2 acres on the east bank of the Kaw River. The first actual Kansas City Livestock Exchange Building was 105 by 127 feet, three stories, of brick with stone trim. It was constructed, at a cost of $35,000, just west of the state line at

When it was built before the Civil War, the Alexander Majors home at 8145 State Line was on 320 acres of land. The original house, as pictured, had nine rooms, each 17' by 17', each with a fireplace.

Alexander Majors' wagon caravans to Santa Fe operated at a time when this area was the western outpost. In his book written in 1893, *Seventy Years on the Frontier*, Majors described a wagon train, "The organization of a full-fledged train for crossing the plains consisted of 25 or 26 large wagons carrying from 3 to 3 1/2 tons each.... The number of cattle (oxen) necessary to draw each wagon was 12, making six yokes or pairs and a prudent freighter would always have 20 to 30 head of extra oxen, in case of accident or lameness.... The men for each train consisted of a wagon master, his assistant, the teamsters, a man to look after the extra cattle and two or three extra men as a reserve...."

Majors got his start in 1848 when he

bought six wagons and oxen. Partnerships were later formed with William H. Russell, a Liberty merchant, and William B. Waddell, a Lexington, Missouri banker.

Today, the Alexander Majors Home has been restored and is open to the public as an historic site.

The newly-constructed twin radio towers of WDAF atop the Kansas City *Star* building are pictured on a 1924 postcard, published in black and white.

Two years earlier, Feb. 17, 1922, a concert had been broadcast as an experiment from the basement. The first studio was a makeshift affair about 15 feet square and consisted of a framework of 2-by-4s covered with burlap cloth. Little was known of soundproofing, so experimentation was the order of the day.

The first broadcast was listened to with crystal sets, some homemade with round oatmeal boxes, according to directions published in the *Star*.

"This being the initial experiment of this kind in Kansas City," said the announcer at the beginning of the program, "the *Star* will appreciate it if those who listen in other towns will notify the *Star* following the concert."

The out of town response was terrific.

The towers were installed in 1924 at a cost of $25,000. They were torn

KANSAS CITY, MO — Home of " The Kansas City Star "

down in the fall of 1942, to be used for scrap steel in the war effort. WDAF and WDAF-TV were sold in 1957.

The editorial prophecies, which had been made on the eve of that first broadcast in 1922 that "the time may be shortly at hand when families will sit home and hear the opera...get farm market reports...clap a receiver to the ear and get the baseball score...listen in to debates in congress," all came true.

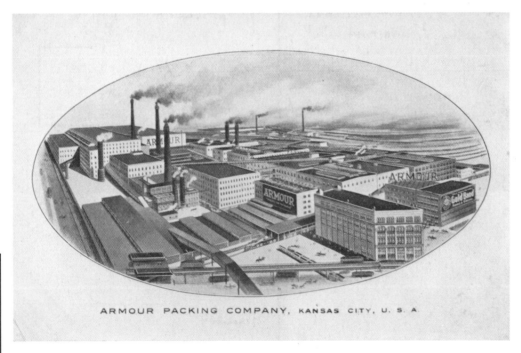

ARMOUR PACKING COMPANY, KANSAS CITY, U. S. A.

California gold-rush history tells of a crude camp of Missourians at Placerville (Hangtown) where a young fellow, Phillip B. Armour, a butcher, had persuaded the small grocery store's owner to let him operate a meat department in the store. It was a novelty, but it did bring in some business. Armour predicted that some day all stores would have meat departments and that if he could make enough money, he planned to butcher and sell meat wholesale to grocery stores.

In Kansas City, at State Line and Central Avenue, a small slaughterhouse was erected by Plankington and Armour in 1871. John Plankington retired in 1885 and Armour Brothers was organized. By 1908, it was one of the largest slaughterhouses in the world.

A feature story in the Kansas City *Journal-Post* of Oct. 16, 1904, used the same oval photograph as the promotional postcard shown. The operations were thus described:

"Five thousand people, men and women all working together under practically one roof and all directed by one man! It is men and the system, humanity and the machine, that makes an enormous business like that of the Armours move like clockwork...."

The big plant extended from the state line west to James Street on the north side of Central Avenue. There were 90 acres of floor space. The firm's business slogan was "Meats for the World."

THE PLAZA, KANSAS CITY, MO.

"The Plaza, Kansas City, Mo." was a small park in the Northeast district, not the Country Club Plaza. It was actually built some twenty years before the Country Club Plaza and was part of the fine residential area on Independence Avenue.

The large red brick building in the background was the old Bonaventure Hotel, built in 1886, at a time when it seemed the city would develop toward the northeast, along the great bluff of the river.

The taller spire in the distance on the card is that of the Independence Avenue Methodist Episcopal Church located at Independence and Olive. Both the hotel and the church have been demolished.

The little Plaza Park of 1.7 acres, acquired by the city in 1898, is said to have cost more per acre than any other city park, since property along Independence Avenue was at peak demand at that time. The park remains today.

Picture postcards were not being made in the United States, nor were they permitted in the mails, when this photograph of 6th and Main Streets was taken in 1871 by W.G. Ragan. When the 1950 Centennial of Kansas City was held, the picture was brought out and widely used.

Marble Hall, on the west side of the street, was a tavern and gambling house, and by "gambling house" as the term went in those days, a faro bank was meant.

Marble Hall, a popular "bank" had a distinguished clientele of Wild Bill Hickok in the '70s and of Bat Masterson, Wyatt Earp, Charlie Basset, Canada Bill, Texas Jack Omahundro and many of the Abilene and Dodge City figures of the early cattle days.

Across the street from Marble Hall, in a rented room on the second floor of the brick building at 509 Main Street, a public library was established and a librarian hired.

It was the city's first public library. The books came from subscription, according to my great-grandfather,

V504 MAIN STREET north from 6th 1871 Kansas City, Mo.

John Taylor, early day builder in Kansas City and one of those who helped gather up the books for the library. Over 2000 volumes were collected.

The name of "Mechanics Institute Library" was taken directly from the Oldham, England Library which John Taylor had known before he came to Missouri in 1849.

In this busy scene from about 1912, looking south from 8th Street on Grand, many of the women shoppers wear long white dresses and summer hats. Men in their shirt sleeves carry their coats. Automobiles have their side curtains down but tops up for protection from the sun.

On the reverse side of this card, published by Hall Brothers, the legend reads, "View of one of the principal thoroughfares of Kansas City showing the Post Office and the Grand Avenue Temple on the left, the Scarritt, Rialto, and Long Buildings on the right."

Grand Avenue, looking South from 8th Street, Kansas City, Mo.

Near 15th Street, Kansas City Mo.

The Blue River at the 15th Street Bridge is pictured on a black and white photographic postcard published early in the century by the North American Post Card Company of Kansas City.

The narrow "tin" bridge was built for horse-and-buggy traffic, but those who used it in later years said that automobile drivers could meet and pass each other, with care.

The many boats banked on the shore of the river attest to the popularity of the place. The steps at the right side led up to the Star Boat Company, owned by James Guinotte. Here canoes, boats, boat repairs, ice cream and cool drinks were furnished to public. A fish bait stand was nearby.

Today, a modern viaduct stands in place of the old bridge.

"Seeing Kansas City" street cars, an attraction for out-of-town visitors and those who wished a scenic ride to view residences and apartments along the city's streets, were much like the regular street cars of the Metropolitan Street Railway System in 1908. The car pictured shows a stop to view "the park."

The special cars were easily identified by signs like the large one in front above the cowcatcher. Tickets were sold for the sightseeing cars at the Owl Drug Store, 920 Main, where the tour started and ended.

J.S. Knight of Kansas City published the card.

A Park View on "Seeing Kansas City" Cars. Operated Daily from Owl Drug Store, 920 Main Street Kansas City, Missouri

J S. KNIGHT, Kansas City, Mo.

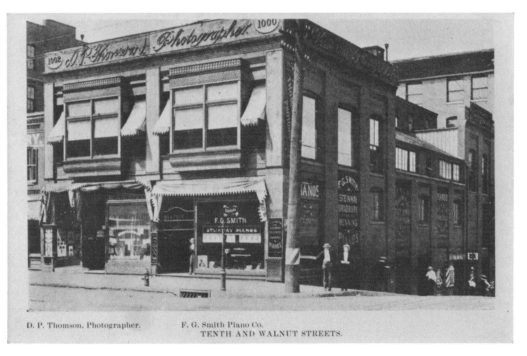

D. P. Thomson, Photographer.   F. G. Smith Piano Co.
TENTH AND WALNUT STREETS.

This store building at 10th and Walnut housed the F.G. Smith Piano Company on the corner and the photo studio of D.P. Thomson next door to the south.

Thomson learned his craft in St. Louis and came here in 1872. He had heard that the Union Pacific wanted a photographer to go with a party to take pictures of the Rocky Mountains for use in the road's advertisements, and he got the job.

A special car had to be fitted here and the party was delayed a week. By week's end, Thomson had looked over the gangling town, visited photographers Merine & Williams, located over the T.M. James Store, bought them out and returned to the Union Pacific official and asked to be released. He told them he had a chance to go into business here and liked the town.

After 50 years here, he had taken over 175,000 photographs of individuals and groups.

Thomson occupied various locations here, first at 6th and Main Street, then 10th and Walnut Street (as pictured), and in 1907 he moved to studios south on Walnut near 12th Street.

He gave his business to George Wolfrom who had been associated with him for over 40 years and Wolfrom continued to operate the business under Thomson's name.

Thomson was a member of the original Priests of Pallas board of directors and was president of the Kansas City Club in 1903.

In the 1930s he presented the Missouri Valley Historical Society with a collection of photographs of pioneers.

Kansas City Fans Getting World Series Returns.

A promotional postcard pictures Kansas City fans getting the World Series returns from a scoreboard on the front of Browning King's men and boys' clothing store at the northeast corner of 11th and Grand.

The postcard was mailed to a Browning King customer July 19, 1924, to advertise a "Genuine Palm Beach suit sale, $11.75, and imported English broadcloth shirts, each $2.45, three for $7."

Since the World Series for 1924 had not been played yet in July, the post card probably pictures the crowd from the previous year. In 1923, the Series was held in New York City with the Yankees beating the New York Giants four out of six games.

Today the old Browning King corner is occupied by office and parking structures.

The Fidelity National Bank Building, 901-13 Walnut, was completed in 1932, becoming the city's second-tallest building at the time, rising 35 stories to a height of 453 feet 9 inches above the sidewalk.

Hoit, Price and Barnes were the architects of the building.

The site is an historic one. Purchased in 1879 by the U.S. Government for a federal building, the massive, gray stone structure housed a post office, U.S. courts, a customs office and other governmental offices. It was completed in the mid-1880s.

The first building had in its twin towers the old town clock and bell, purchased by public-spirited citizens because there was no U.S. appropriation at the time for the clock and bell. The clock was said to be the largest clock west of the Mississippi. The old bell first rang in the new year of 1884.

President Cleveland, the first U.S. President to visit Kansas City, spoke from the balcony of the historic structure to a crowd of 5000. He made the oft-quoted statement, "There is no limit to what a community living in such a place, and actuated by such a spirit, can do."

In 1902, the federal government built a new post office at 9th and Grand, and sold the old three-story building to the Fidelity Trust Company, which used the location until it was outgrown. Then in 1929 the Trust Company decided to raze the building and build the current skyscraper. The new design, however, incorporated the twin tower motif.

In 1931, as the new bank building neared completion, the old clock was installed in the twin towers, the four faces looking out over the city in four directions.

In 1946, the federal government bought the Fidelity Bank Building, but by the 1950s, the clock was turned off. In August 1972, fearing the stained glass face of the clock might fall into the street, it was dismantled.

The message on this promotional postcard might have been true in 1909, when Kansas City had seven overall manufacturers and all of their customers were male. But not today.

The postcard, printed in dark blue, was a Fitz souvenir distributed by the dry goods manufacturers, Burnham, Munger & Root from their wholesale house at 8th and Broadway. The factory where Fitz overalls were made was just east at 8th and May.

THIS WORLD IS MADE UP OF THREE KINDS OF PEOPLE

THOSE WHO DO   THOSE WHO DON'T   THOSE WHO CAN'T

WEAR **FITZ** OVERALLS

FITZ SOUVENIR

Greetings
Delighted
Feeling O.K.
Great Show
Miss You
Fine Town
Big Time
Pretty Girls
Regards
Much Love
Good Bye

LARGEST APARTMENT HOUSE IN KANSAS CITY   WALKER PLACE   8th & Highland Kansas City, U.S.A.

The Walker Place, an ornate apartment of the late Victorian period, is pictured on a black and white postcard. It was located at 8th and Highland.

The 4-story Queen Anne style structure, with an onion dome atop the corner tower and a porch for each apartment, was originally called the Quinlan Block and was built by Judge C.C. Quinlan, an early day livestock man.

Quinlan came to Kansas City in 1873 and became a member of the livestock commission firm of Quinlan, Montgomery & Company. He was so successful that he was known as one of the wealthiest of the men who accumulated fortunes through handling cattle.

The Quinlan Block was built during the building boom of the late 1880s and is first shown on municipal plat books of 1891. The Judge invested heavily in real estate, but when he suffered reverses in real estate and cattle, the building passed into other hands, then becoming Walker Place.

The Walker was similar in appearance to other large apartments built in that fashionable northeast neighborhood. All were later demolished.

Rock Hill Boulevard, Kansas City.

Through an opening in the trees lining Rockhill Road, motorists could catch a glimpse of Oak Hall, the beautiful rambling limestone residence of William Rockhill Nelson, founder of the *Kansas City Star*, and his family.

Mr. Nelson, who was a builder before becoming a newspaperman, used to say, "The great danger in building large houses is that they look like a palace or like a public institution. I have tried to build mine like a home."

In a bequest which left in trust all he owned (after the death of his wife and daughter) to the people of Kansas City for an art gallery, he stipulated Oak Hall be razed and the grounds used for the new building.

Only the library from Oak Hall was retained. It was built into an upper floor exhibit. The room, containing the original wood paneling, floors, rugs, furniture, pictures, and books, is viewed by thousands of visitors to the Nelson-Atkins Museum of Art.

The Home of the Kansas City Star, Kansas City, Mo.

The sixth (and present) home of the Kansas City *Star*, an Italian Renaissance building of tapestry brick, appears on an early postcard much as when it was completed in 1911, at 18th and Grand Ave.

William Rockhill Nelson, the founder and owner of the newspaper, related that he got his inspiration for the building from the McLean Home in Washington.

Jarvis Hunt, eminent architect from Chicago, was entrusted with the design of the building. Hunt would later design the Union Station.

Hunt's first plans for the building, a palatial structure in marble, were rejected in no uncertain terms by Nelson, "A beautiful building of course, but it wouldn't do for a print shop. You couldn't imagine a printer's devil all covered with ink come running out of a marble palace."

The adaptation of the McLean Home was then worked out by Hunt under Nelson's supervision.

Scarritt Point, North Terrace Park, Kansas City, Mo.

Three women wearing large hats and skirts sweeping the ground appear in the postcard scene of Scarritt Point in North Terrace Park. Heim's Brewery, in the right foreground, appears to be almost as tall as the cliff beside it.

The park, one of the oldest in the city, contained 308 acres of land and was acquired in nine different tracts between 1885 and 1920, at a total cost of $1,032,000.

North Terrace Park was renamed Kessler Park honoring George E. Kessler, who was largely responsible for much of the early planning of the parks and boulevards system.

Scarritt Point was named for the Rev. Nathan Scarritt.

Back in 1902, John L. and Jacob S. Loose, along with John H. Wiles, formed the Loose-Wiles Biscuit Company. Early Kansas City directories list them as "Cracker & Candy Mfgrs., Takoma Biscuit, Crackers, Candy, etc., 8th, Santa Fe and Henning Streets, K.C., Mo."

This promotional postcard was mailed with a 1-cent green stamp by T. Ellers, a candy salesman for the company, to his customers, Carl & Hunter at Gas, Kan. The card announced the date when a call would be made to obtain an order.

The card pictured 12 workmen with long white aprons and rolled up sleeves ready for work in the peanut candy department. Great copper kettles with gas burners for cooking the sugar are at the right side and slabs at the left hold fresh batches of the finished product. Large buckets in the aisle hold shelled peanuts.

One of the principal products of Loose-Wise was a cracker, marketed under the name of Sunshine Biscuits. Sunshine became a well-known name, and in 1947, Loose-Wiles officials decided on a change of name because Sunshine was better known.

30 Views in Loose-Wiles Factory—No. 14. Peanut Candy Dept.

Kansas City had two separate telephone companies when this photographic postcard was made in 1909. Each had separate offices, exchanges, telephone poles and personnel. Both systems had long distance service.

Residents decided which company they preferred, while most business houses had both. It was an aggravation to phone a new acquaintance and discover he or she did not have a phone hookup with the same company.

The Home Telephone Company Building was at 1018 Baltimore, as pictured. The Adams Express Company offices were next door.

Home Company records showed 20,146 telephones in use for the year ending March 31, 1908. The Bell Telephone Company reported 20,000 instruments in use the same year.

Long distance connections were located on the top floor of the building pictured, according to Elizabeth Wagner, a telephone information operator at the time. She said she received $28.50 and later $30 a month, with no days off. One day she was called to the office of the supervisor, a Mrs. King, and was rebuked for having been seen walking at noon on the 11th with one of the men supervisors of the company. A Home Company rule forbade fraternization between men employees and the telephone girls, a rule supposedly for better discipline.

The Home Telephone Company and the Bell System merged in 1919. Regulatory bodies agreed the transaction was to the best interests of the public.

Home Telephone Bldg. K.C. Mo. -662

Y. M. C. A. Building, Kansas City, Mo.

The Young Men's Christian Association was founded in 1844.

In 1860, a unit was established in Kansas City under the leadership of Rev. W.M. Leftwich, who emphasized that "Kansas City was subject to many demoralizing influences," and that the Y.M.C.A. would have a beneficial effect.

The Kansas City organization, like many others, suffered a setback during the Civil War, but it soon after revived and occupied two buildings it owned at 10th and Walnut and at 9th and Locust.

In 1906, Henry M. Beardsley, a councilman and later mayor, declared the Kansas City organization could raise $250,000 in 30 days. The drive raised $283,000 and the building at 10th and Oak, as pictured, was the result. Charles Smith, a Kansas City architect, was the designer.

The Y was formally opened in January 1910, with an indoor swimming pool, track, cafeteria, night study classes, bowling alleys, chapel, game rooms, and a clubroom for underprivileged boys. One of the early residents of the Y building was Joyce Hall, founder of Hallmark Cards.

The 1908 photographic postcard of an 8-year-old Kansas City *Star* newsboy was made at the Eastern Photo Post Card Company, 204 E. 12th, one of the 12th Street shops popular with visitors.

Patrons were photographed in a balloon basket in the safety of the studio. A painted backdrop with a panorama of downtown Kansas City gave the illusion of being aloft over the city.

Pictured on this card was Eugene Steinkraus, who sold his papers in front of the Emery-Bird-Thayer store.

A few years later, Eugene was called the "Flying Dutchman" when he played on the Manual Training High School football team and was a member of the city all-star team.

This early promotional postcard, lithographed in color in Berlin, reads:

"Residence, Office and Consultation Rooms of Dr. C.H. Carson, Founder of the Carson College of Psychic-Sarcology and School of Vital Science, North East Corner of Washington and 12th Streets, Kansas City, Mo. The Temple of Health, where all diseases are treated successfully without drugs, medicines, electricity, or surgical operations."

Dr. Carson's method of treatment gave the patients lessons in breathing, exercise, food, clothing, etc. Massage with warm olive oil was given. A photograph from a 1902 brochure of Kansas City scenes and businesses shows one corner of his office filled with the crutches of patients presumably cured.

Dr. Carson had practiced in Kansas City for 30 years before an attempt by the state board of health to close the institution.

An article from the November 30, 1910 Kansas City *Journal* details the close of the case by the Missouri State Supreme Court when it handed down a decision in favor of Dr. Carson.

Residence, Office and Consultation Rooms of Dr. C. H. Carson, Founder of the Carson College of Psychic-Sarcology and School of Vital Science. North East Corner of Washington and 12th Streets, Kansas City, Mo. The Temple of Health, where all diseases are treated successfully without drugs, medicines, electricity, or surgical operations.

A photographic postcard of an important downtown corner, Eleventh and Baltimore, is shown on this 1908 image labeled "Looking east on 11th from Fire Department."

Six firemen with fire equipment and horses are pictured opposite the Willis Wood Theater, which shows interesting architectural detail by its designer, Louis S. Curtiss.

The Hotel Continental later occupied the site.

The tower on the tall brick building in the center of the picture is that of the old George B. Peck department store, later razed for a parking lot and restaurant.

The Darby Corporation built and launched an ocean-going vessel a day for the U.S. Navy during World War II. Two thousand ships were built and went down the ways at the confluence of the Missouri and Kaw Rivers. They made the 1000-mile trip to the Gulf of Mexico, where they were sent in convoys to points all over the world.

After the war, Harry Darby told the story of a crisis early in January, 1944. It was recounted in *City of the Future* by Haskell and Fowler.

"Sixty barges built in Greater Kansas City and Leavenworth were tied up at Darby's docks by low water. Navy officials in Washington were frantic at the delay.

The admirals looked at the map, saw Ft. Peck Dam far up the river in Montana and ordered the water released. The water soaked along its way to K.C. but when it finally arrived the net effect on the river was 1 inch.

The screams were heard all the way from Washington. Then came the grotesque order to put the big ocean-going ships on wheels. The L.C.T.s [Landing Craft Tanks] were wider than the highway, but wheels were provided. On second thought it occurred to local naval officers that they couldn't get through the bridge structures (because the barges were wider than the bridges). To that the high command responded with the order to cut off the bridge structures, tear out the bridges and build temporary replacements, if necessary. Anything! Move the barges. Somebody was in a whale of a rush over something...

Just one day before the demolition was to start, clouds rolled out of the west and the rains came. The river rose 4 feet almost overnight. Wheels were jerked away and the barges slid into the water....

The following June 6 the reason for the frantic orders became clear. It was D Day. Midwestern barges were hitting the beaches of Normandy.

Three times during the war the Darby Corporation and the men and women employees were awarded the "E" flag of three stars, the highest award given by the Army and Navy for war production effort.

The New Kansas City Club, Kansas City.

Gentlemen who lived on old Quality Hill were sometimes scolded by their wives for smoking cigars in their homes. So a small group decided to rent a room at the Coates House, about a block away, so they could be at peace while they enjoyed their after-dinner cigars.

As the gathering place became more popular, the group expanded, and in November 1882, rented club headquarters in a converted store building at the corner of Broadway and 11th. This was the beginning of the Kansas City Club.

There were 42 charter members, among them the Coates, Askews, Armours, Bullenes, Fosters and other representatives of old city families. Col. A.A. Tomlinson was the first president. Early on, it was determined that political discussion should never be allowed to dominate the club life.

Membership grew rapidly and by 1885 more commodious quarters were needed. A site at the northeast corner of 12th and Wyandotte was purchased for $42,000 and a 5-story building costing $70,000 was completed and occupied in 1887.

Shown on the postcard is the third and final home of the Club, a $2,500,000 building at 13th and Baltimore. Work on the 14-story steel frame of the structure was begun in April 1919. Construction had been interrupted by the World War restrictions on building.

The big cream terra cotta building is of English Tudor Gothic design. The architects were Smith, Rea and Lovitt. The deep excavation for foundations was blasted through solid rock.

The "new" Kansas City Club, as it was called at the time, formally opened with a dinner dance May 19, 1922. 1500 guests attended.

The grand opening of Kansas City's horse racing track, Elm Ridge, a block east of The Paseo between 59th and 63rd Streets, was April 28, 1904. Considered far out in the country at the time and on a site chosen for its vista of woods and gently rolling hills, it compared favorably with many race tracks in the country.

In the picture is the original clubhouse of native stone, with spacious porches, the paddock and grandstand seating 1500.

The track operated only two years, when the sport was outlawed by the State of Missouri. The next few years, the facility was used for athletic events, motor car and motorcycle racing.

The Blue Hills Club, organized in 1912 with 670 members, was the next occupant of the site. More recently, part of the site was taken for construction of the Metro Plaza shopping center.

Elm Ridge Race Track and Club House, Kansas City, Mo.

Mystery Team?

The photographic postcard showing nine baseball players and their manager is titled "Kansas City Red Sox – at Uniontown, Kan., Oct. 10, 1913."

Files of the *Star* of October 10 and the day after have no mention of the game or the Red Sox team.

A telephone call to Uniontown, Kansas disclosed the fact that old files were not available to reveal who won the game (if there was one) and to identify the players.

An old-time baseball fan suggested this Red Sox team might have been one of the many teams sponsored by the Kansas City Athletic Club. These teams were semiprofessional. They were unpaid, with the possible exception of the pitchers.

– Kansas City Red Sox – At Uniontown Ks   10/10/13

Frank C. Brown, a member of Kansas City's first motorcycle squad, wore his blue serge uniform, along with leather leggings, cap and goggles. There were no windshields on motorcycles in 1909. Beside him in this postcard picture is his new Indian cycle with carbide headlights.

He was standing in front of his parents' home in a section of the city known as "Dutch Hill" at 2726 Cherry. The right side of the double house, 2744 Cherry, was used by the Watson Bakery Company which had baking ovens in a building at the rear. Barns housed wagons and horses for delivering the bakery goods.

Frank's father, Aquilla (Pop) Brown, leaning on the porch post, was listed in the 1907 City Directory as vice-president of the bakery and James Watson was listed as president. Pop, in his horsedrawn vehicle, was a familiar figure on his bread delivery route.

The blond, boyish idol of the American public, Charles Lindbergh, stole the show at the dedication of Kansas City's airport, August 17, 1927.

By midmorning on dedication day spectators were heading for the field on foot or by special busses which carried them from 5th and Broadway.

At 2 p.m., on schedule, Lindbergh's plane circled the business district and headed for the airport. In his short address at the dedication stand he praised the accessibility of the field, saying it was nearer the heart of the city than any he knew except those in Brussels and Paris.

After the ceremonies Lindbergh rode through the streets packed with cheering crowds, over one of the longest parade routes in the history of the city.

The 17 merchants who ran a 1/2 page sketch of Lindbergh in the *Times* expressed the feelings of Kansas Citians in the few lines below his picture. They wrote:

"Welcome Lindy"

"By your bravery, courtesy and modesty you have won everlasting fame and honor for your nation, your state and your profession. We are proud to welcome you to Kansas City."

A photographic postcard taken in Kansas City September 1, 1910, shows Theodore Roosevelt being driven down Grand Avenue in an open carriage. A huge bouquet of roses lay near the former President who is standing in the carriage tipping his hat.

That day's issue of the Kansas City *Star* reported: "Thousands stand without umbrellas to see the ex-President pass through the streets." (Being considerate of those standing behind). There was a big jam at the depot. Every bit of space in the old building was filled with "Teddy Boosters."

After the ride through the downtown district, a luncheon was held at the Baltimore Hotel. Members of the orchestra, who had braved the rain to furnish the music, played and sang a parody of "Kelly," a popular song of the day:

Has anybody here seen Teddy?
He's from Oyster Bay.
His head is clear and heart is true
He's insurgent through and

through.
Has anybody here seen Teddy?
He is on his way.
That night, 20,000 persons packed Convention Hall to hear Roosevelt.

The Kansas City *Times* of September 2 called it a "strong speech," and said, "the Progressive Party leader gave voice to sentiments that made him a popular idol."

The Scarritt Building, pictured on this 1907 postcard, had just recently been completed, joining the R.A. Long Building and the National Bank of Commerce in the immediate vicinity as new skyscrapers. It was built by the Scarritt Estate Company (formed in 1903) which was composed of six children of the prominent early-day Kansas Citian, Nathan Scarritt, who arrived in the area in 1848 as teacher and preacher.

Scarritt had owned much city property by the time of his death in 1899. His farm holdings included the homestead, bounded by a rail fence north of what is now St. John in northeast Kansas City, and extending to the bluff and what is now Van Brunt Boulevard. Scarritt Point lay on the western boundary. He also owned land at 25th and Grand.

The fireproof Scarritt Building, erected at a cost of $750,000, had entrances on Grand and 9th and on Walnut through the 4-story Scarritt Arcade. The "H" shaped design of architects Root and Siemens was done to let in more light. Over the years, the office building was occupied by the Kansas City Gas Company, the Scarritt Estate Company and others. The Scarritt Building and Scarritt Arcade have just recently undergone extensive historic restoration, recapturing much of the original splendor.

Scarritt Building, Kansas City.

Grand Central Station, at the foot of Wyandotte at 2nd, was built by 1890 by the Kansas City, Pittsburg and Gulf Railway, now the Kansas City Southern.

H.C. Lindsay and F.W. Martin planned and constructed the building for Arthur E. Stilwell, railroad builder of the early days. It was considered a model depot at the time and the pride of railroad men. The cost was $65,000

Stilwell's greatest triumph was building the line from Kansas City, through Arkansas and Louisiana to Port Arthur, Tex. The town bears his given name.

The Kansas City Southern used the old station until it moved to the new Union Station in 1914.

The building was razed by men from the Helping Hand Institute in November, 1932.

6843. THE WEST BOTTOMS, KANSAS CITY, MO.

From Tunnel

An elevated railroad connected Kansas City, the old Union Depot in the West Bottoms and Kansas City, Kansas. It was the first elevated line constructed outside New York City, and was called the Wyandotte and Tunnel Railway.

The line began at 8th and Delaware in Kansas City and is shown on the old photographic postcard as the tracks entered the 8th Street tunnel. It continued to Union Depot and, by elevated tracks, to 5th and Central in Kansas City, Kansas.

The tunnel was completed April 21, 1888, by the railroad and tunnel builder, D.M. Edgerton, and was the answer of the brilliant young Kansas City engineer, Robert Gillham, to the problem of getting to the Union Depot from the city's high bluffs above. The tunnel was finished in a year's time at a cost of $800,000, a huge amount of money in 1888.

The east entrance to the tunnel in 1888 was at 8th and Washington but in 1903 was changed to 8th and Broadway, with the grade reduced.

Trains ran every 4 minutes in each direction. The fare was 5 cents.

Dear Friend:

Having visited the two places of which Kansas City is proud, I take pleasure in sending you this Souvenir card.

Sincerely

Edgar & Pauline.

CONVENTION HALL.

ARMOUR PACKING CO.
MEATS FOR THE WORLD.
KANSAS CITY, U.S.A.

PLANT OF THE ARMOUR PACKING CO.

FLOOR SPACE
90 ACRES.

The card, a collector's item whose reverse side bears the heading announcing the first legal status of the picture postcard in the United States, called the attention of the postmaster and the sender to the fact that a 1-cent stamp was necessary and that it was not the usual regulation prepaid government 1-cent postcard.

The two places depicted "of which Kansas City is proud" were the Convention Hall and the plant of Armour & Co. with a "floor space of 90 acres."

This 1914 photographic postcard pictures the narrowest of early downtown Kansas City office buildings, the 8-story Victor Building at the northwest corner of 10th and Main. The building had a 27 and 1/2 foot frontage on Main and 129 feet on 10th. The entrance to the building was on 10th.

Victor H. Laederich built the unusual structure at a spot where early plotters had left a jog in 10th Street and, in so doing, he brought together two leases on two narrow strips of land. He proceeded to erect the tall, narrow building, referred to in early news stories as the "toothpick building."

The fireproof structure was erected in 1908 at a cost of $200,000. Corridors had marble floors and marble wainscotting to the height of 7 feet. There were 75 offices in the "toothpick", many of them occupied by realtors.

The Valerius Cafe, with its entrance on 10th Street, occupied basement space and was especially popular as a businessman's luncheon spot.

The Victor was razed in June, 1965. The space is now covered with highrise office space.

NICOLL THE TAILOR

389-VICTOR BUILDING

The privately published postcard was now allowed the same message privileges and rates as the government-issued plain cards. They were to be approximately the same size, weight and quality and titled 'Private Mailing Card.'

This signaled the beginning of the flood of private postcard publishers and the repoduction of colorful street scenes, parks, buildings, vehicles, and people of fashion. The collecting craze was on.

PRIVATE MAILING CARD.

AUTHORIZED BY ACT OF CONGRESS
MAY 19TH 1898.
THIS SIDE IS EXCLUSIVELY FOR
THE ADDRESS.

PUT
ONE CENT
STAMP
HERE.

J.C. Nichols' housing development in Kansas City, Rockhill Park, in part, covered the area from Fifty-third to Fifty-fifth Streets and from Brookside Boulevard to Main. The scene on this promotional postcard published in 1917 was looking east on Fifty-third.

The car halted on the roadway is Nichols' who was making an inspection tour of the construction work when the photograph was taken.

The car, a 1909 Stevens-Duryea made in Chicopee Falls, Massachusetts, was driven by Ernest O. Holt. In the rear seat were the three Nichols children: Miller, Eleanor and Jesse Clyde, Jr.

Holt, the family chauffeur, came from the Black Forest country in Germany, and he lived with the Nichols family 25 years. He retired in 1927 and later resided in South Laguna, California. Holt identified the car pictured and added in a letter to the author:

"As a rule, most mornings, Mr. Nichols would go over the new construction with Mr. Linscott, before heading for his office downtown. As a rule, we never took the children around except on Sundays. Also, we

Development Work in Rockhill Park and Country Side. — 1,000 Acres Restricted.

never knew when we would get back as usually there was a lot of measuring and walking, sometimes through mud. I always carried an extra pair of shoes in the car for change.

Mr. Nichols would meet Mr. Linscott in his Model T Ford coupe and there were appointments with prospects and also with Herb Hare, landscape architect, in whom Mr. Nichols placed great faith in the layouts. [He met] also with Mr. George Kessler of the St. Louis park board, who was advisor to the Kansas City park board, especially to Mr. A.R. Meyer, first park board president."

Kansas City, Mo.   1522 Loretto Academy

Lawn Tennis Court.   Basket Ball grounds.

Loretto Academy. Kansas City, Mo.

Dear Ethel —
Why in the world dont you girls
write to me,
                        Lovingly Genevieve

In 1901, the Sisters of Loretto purchased five acres on Broadway near 35th and the residence belonging formerly to Colonel E.S. Jewett. The home was converted into the convent but was quickly outgrown.

In September, 1902, Mother M. Prexedes Carty purchased a tract of land at 39th and Roanoke Parkway and, soon after, the first sod was turned for the foundation of the large new building as pictured in this 1905 postcard.

Upon laying the cornerstone in 1903, Bishop Glennon said that the dedication was a fulfillment of a dream of earlier Lorettines when they passed through Kansas City a half century before to spread their faith in the newly-opened West.

The completed school, symbol of this devotion, offered instruction in piano, harp, violin, and vocal music. The Fine Arts Department was notable along with other academic areas.

The school later moved to a 38 acre site on Wornall Road at 124th. The venerable red brick building on 39th was sold to Calvary Bible College in 1964. The small trees shown in the picture tower over the building which remains today.

The 12th Street scene of 1909, looking west in the upper card, shows street car tracks, horse and wagon traffic and early-day establishments. The view was incorrectly marked as the "300 Block 12th St."

Actually the 400 block is in the foreground, the block now occupied by the Jackson County Courthouse and the City Hall. Today, street car tracks have been removed and the street widened. Traffic is one-way east.

The 1909 City Directory identifies occupants of the block as: White Sewing Machine Co., 423 E. 12th, George M. Hughes, Mgr.; Japanese Store; Furnished Rooms, Emil Scharnagel, 417 E. 12th (later that year the building became the Lee Hotel). Postcards, 411 E. 12th, Samuel Kaplan. On the other side of the street was: Pool, 416 E. 12th and the Newport Billiard Hall, 414 E. 12th.

The true "300 Block" shows two men and a waiting horse-drawn street cab in front of Thomas W. Johnson's saloon, in the left foreground of this scene. The saloon's site and the remainder of the block are now occupied by the Public Library.

The picture looks west and the Baltimore Hotel is seen on the right of the street in the distance. The "300" banners were hung overhead to publicize a 300-block festival.

❖ Index ❖